Sean Kenney

Cool Cars and Trucks

Christy Ottaviano Books
Henry Holt and Company
New York

For Lily

Henry Holt and Company, LLC
Publishers since 1866
175 Fifth Avenue
New York, New York 10010
www.HenryHoltKids.com

Library of Congress Cataloging-in-Publication Data
Kenney, Sean.
Sean Kenney's cool cars / Sean Kenney.
p. cm.
ISBN 978-0-8050-8761-1
1. Automobiles—Models—Juvenile literature. 2. LEGO toys—
Juvenile literature. I. Title. II. Title: Cool cars.
TL237.K46 2009
730.92—dc22
2008036812

First Edition—2009
Printed in December 2009 in the United States of America by Worzalla Publishing Company Inc.,
Stevens Point, Wisconsin, on acid-free paper. ∞

5 7 9 10 8 6 4

LEGO bricks were used to create the models for this book.
The models were photographed by John E. Barrett.

Let's build some cars!

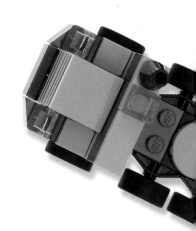

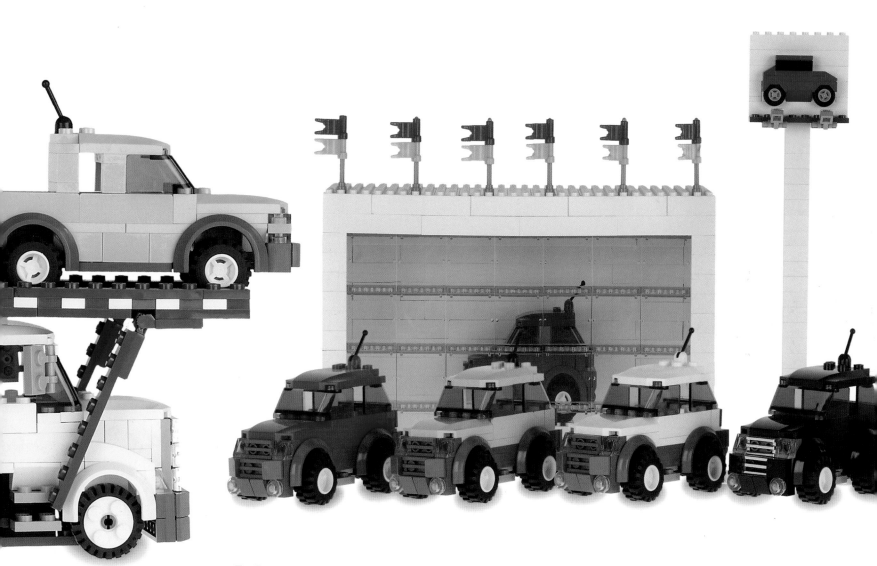

Here come the cool cars!

A big car carrier brings lots of cars and trucks to the auto dealership.

SUV

1

2

3

1	3
2	4

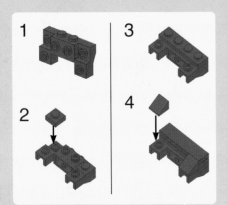

4

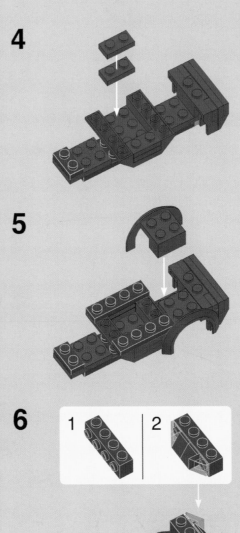

5

6

1	2

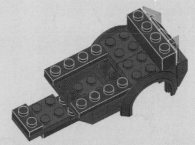

7

8

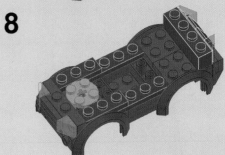

9

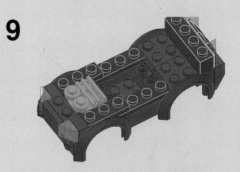

10

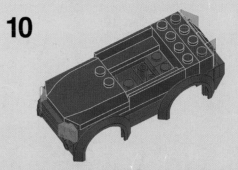

6

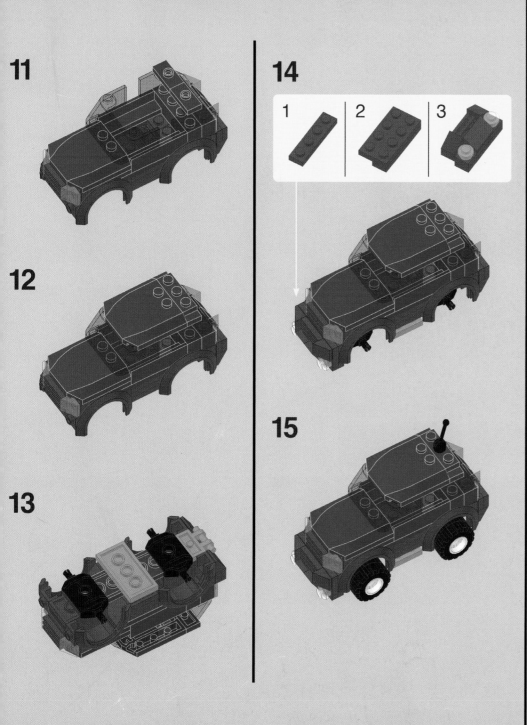

11

12

13

14

| 1 | 2 | 3 |

15

Can you change the SUV to look like these cars?

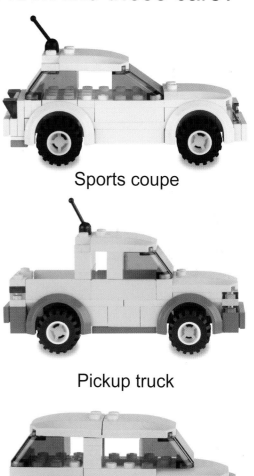

Sports coupe

Pickup truck

Minivan

Taxis of all sizes

If you don't have enough LEGO
pieces to build a big car, try
making the same car
in a smaller size.

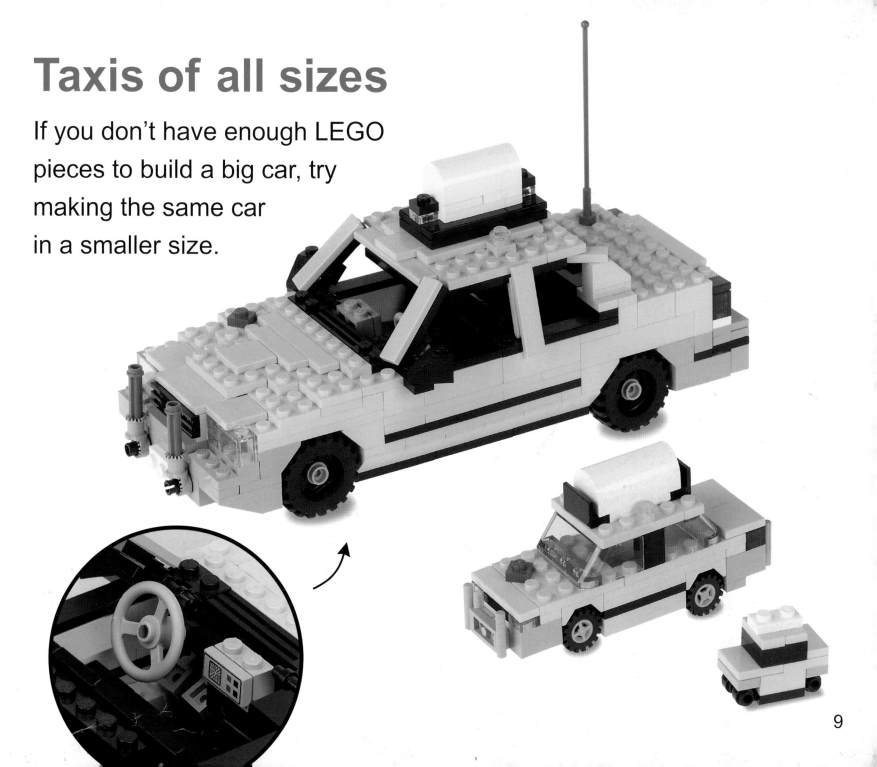

Too fast!

Sporty cars can drive fast but speeders better watch out.

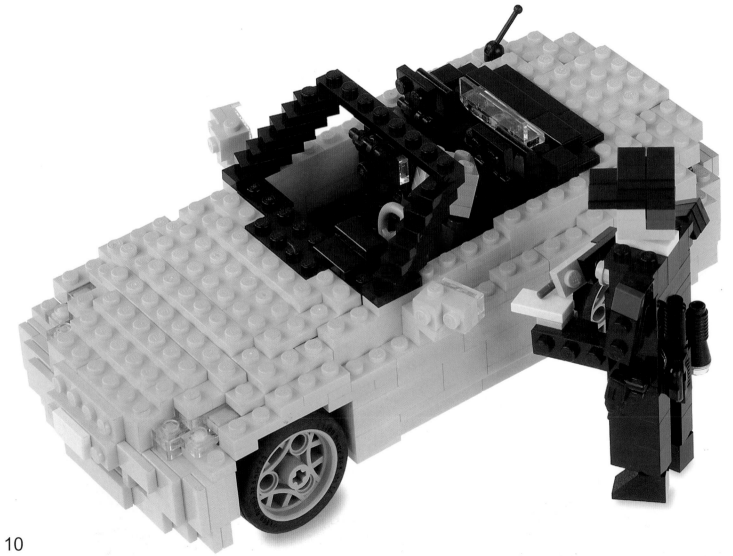

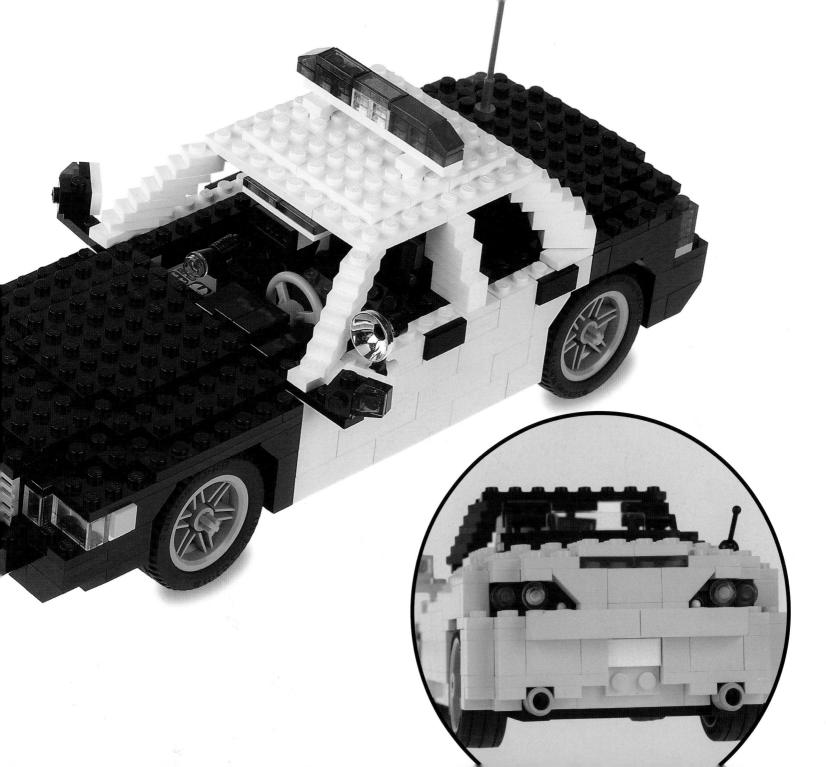

Load the airplane

These tough little airport vehicles have to hurry to get passengers and luggage onto the plane in time for takeoff.

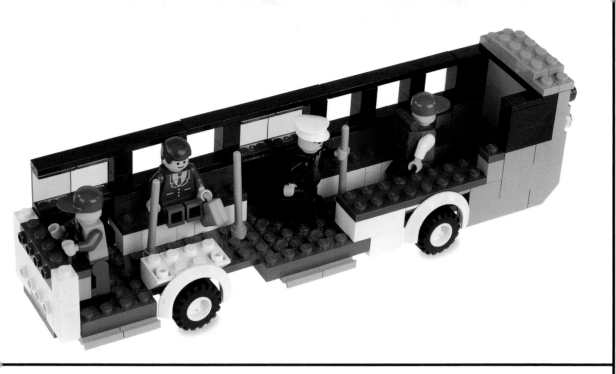

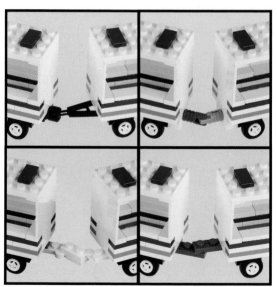

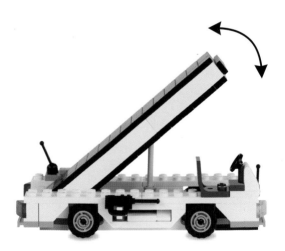

Try different hinges.

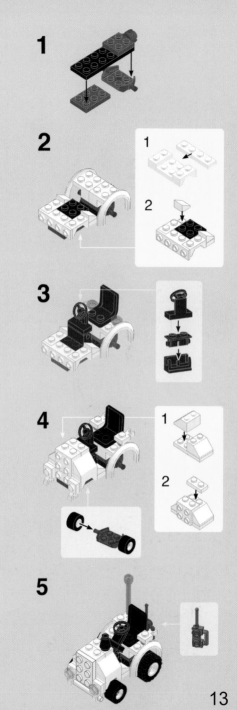

1

2

3

4

5

13

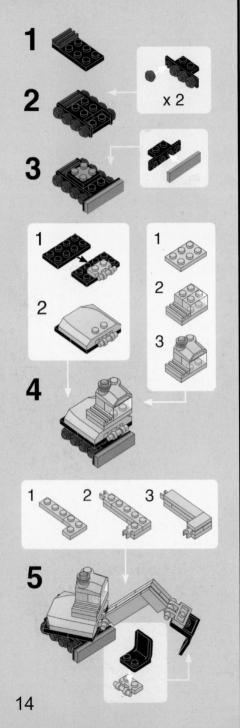

Strong builders and heavy haulers

Strong trucks move lots of dirt, rocks, cement, and steel to help construct buildings.

Pocket-sized crazy cars

You need only a few wheels and some little pieces to build a turbocharged racing machine.

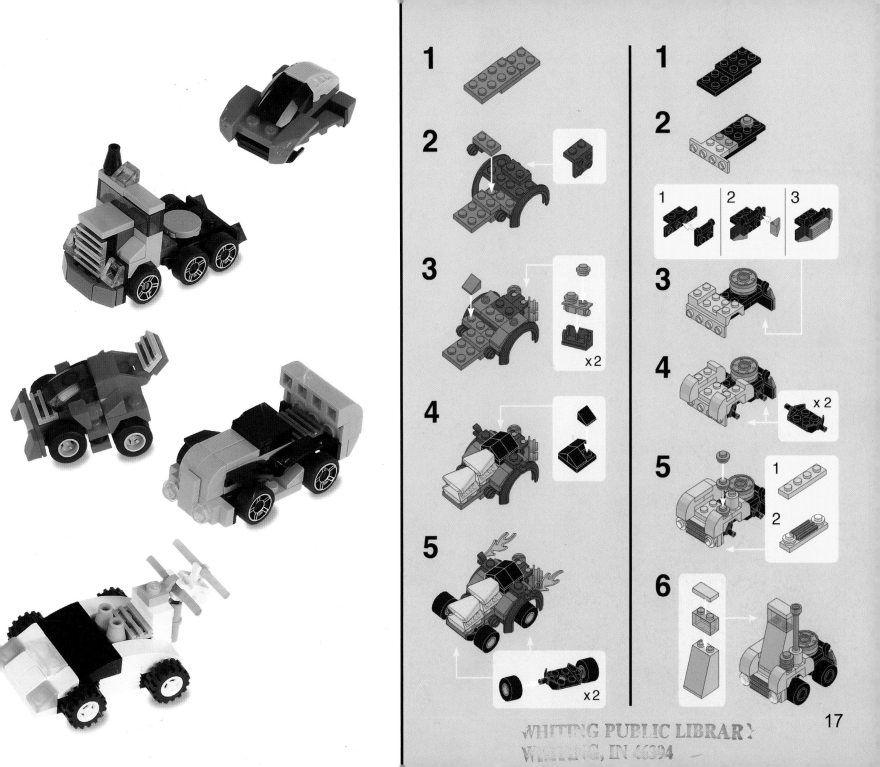

Rush to the rescue!

Fire trucks, police cars, and ambulances hurry off to save people's lives.

19

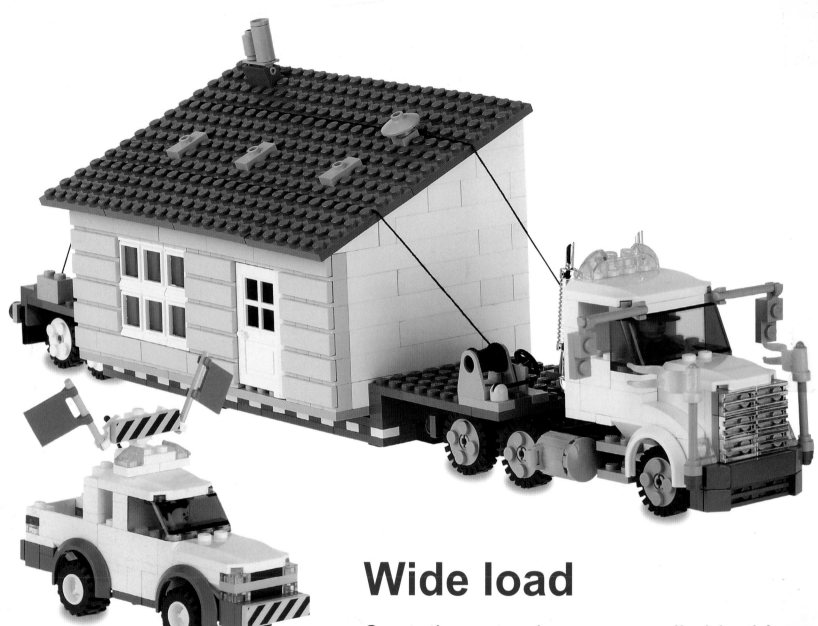

Wide load

Sometimes trucks move really big things, like a house!

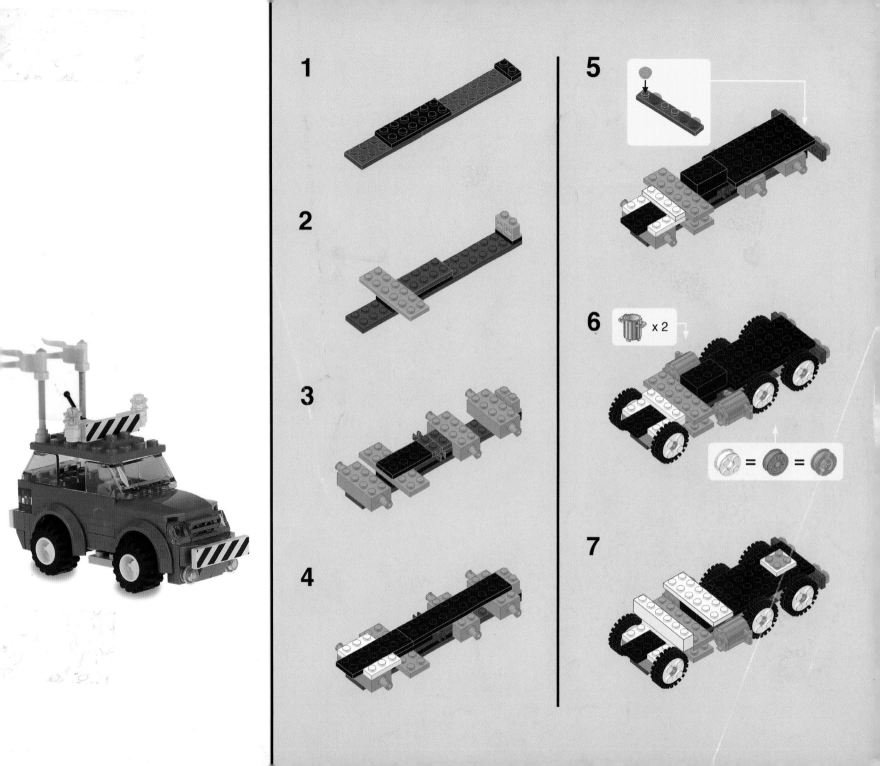

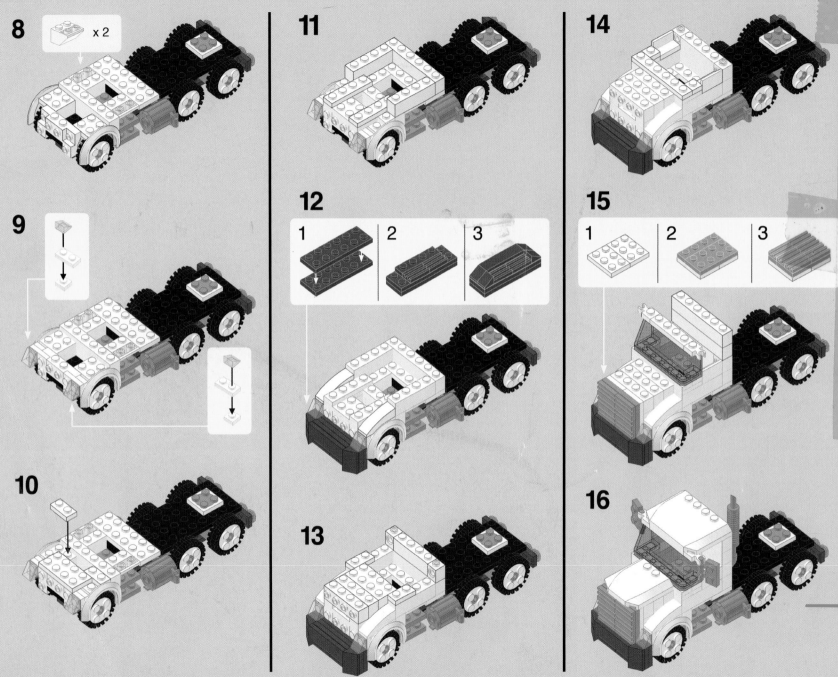

8 x 2

9

10

11

12
1 2 3

13

14

15
1 2 3

16

Make your own truck

You can use the same basic design to create many other trucks.

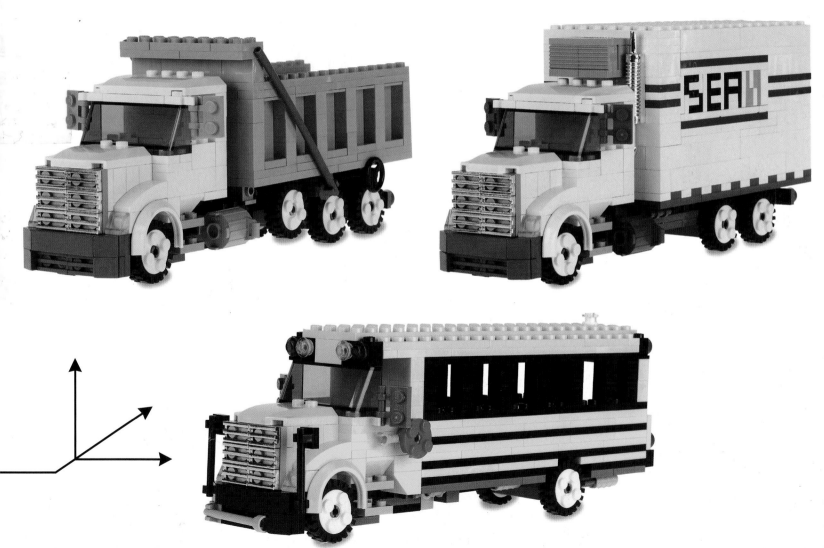

What other kinds of furniture can you make?

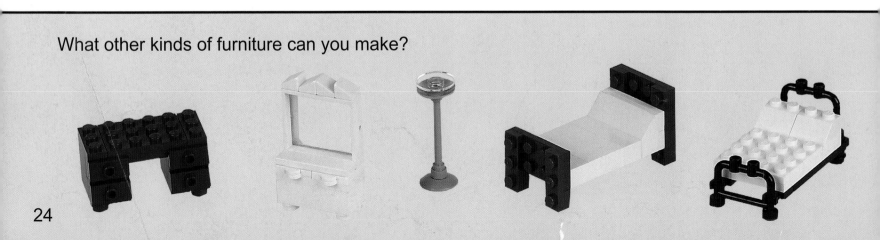

Moving day

A moving truck with a ramp and lots of doors makes it easy to carry furniture and boxes to a new house.

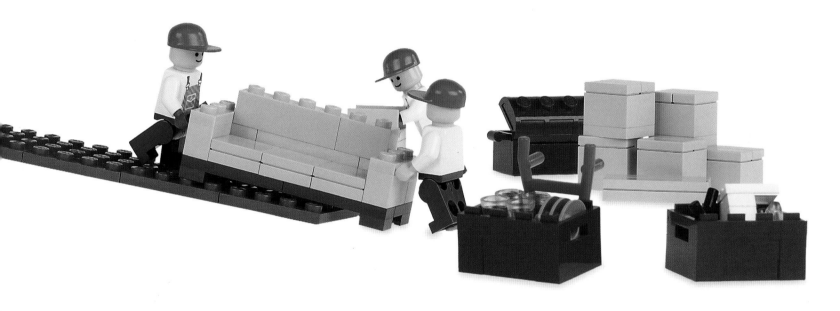

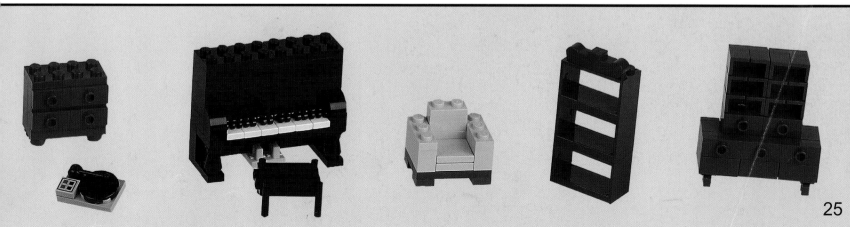

Around your neighborhood

Every day, cool cars are all around, bringing packages, fixing your street, even selling ice cream!

Tune it up

Switch out engines, fenders, wheels, and more to turn a regular car into a street racer.

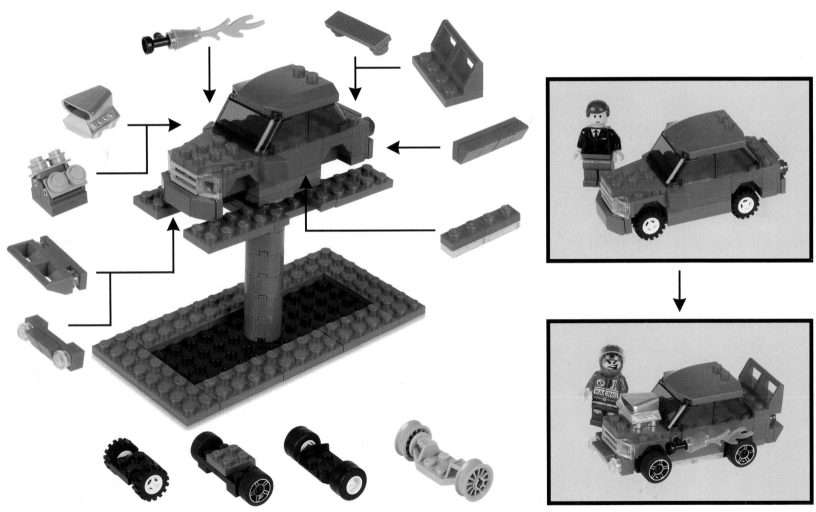

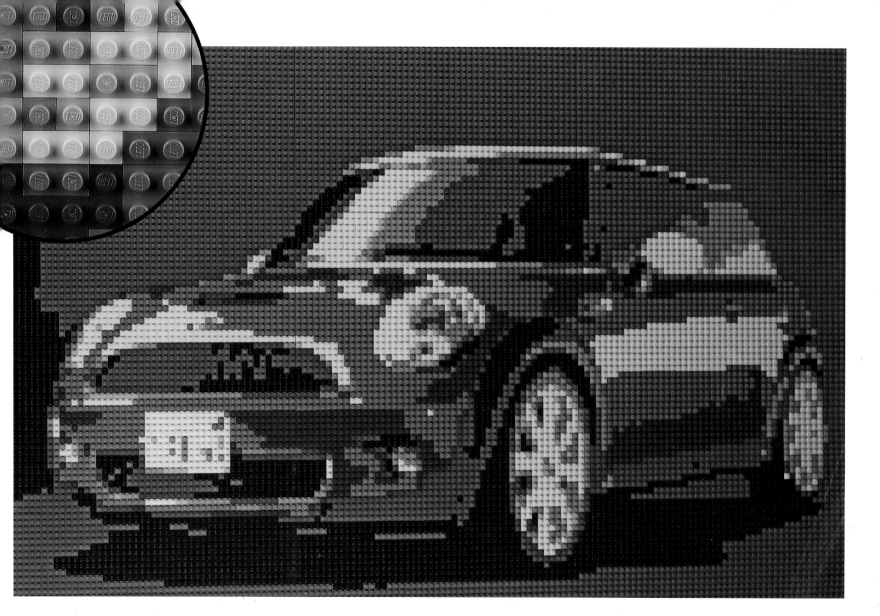

Flatten it down

Build a mosaic by creating a flat picture of a car.

Build it BIG!

Create giant versions of LEGO bricks,
then combine them into a giant car.

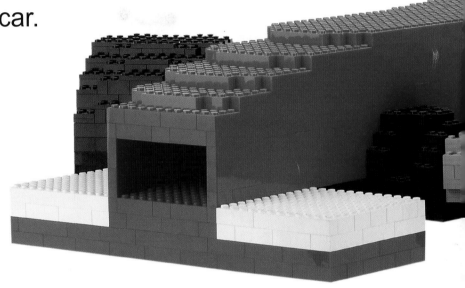

These large bricks are 6 times the size of regular bricks.

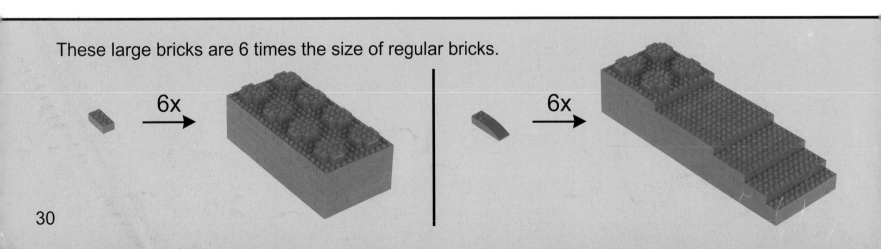

6x

6x

6x

6x

About Sean

Sean Kenney likes to prove you can build anything with LEGO bricks. He makes LEGO sculptures and models at his studio in New York City.

Sean picked up his first LEGO bricks as a child, and his passion for LEGO grew through the years as he grew. He is now recognized as one of the premier LEGO brick builders in the world.

Visit Sean at http://www.seankenney.com to:

- Share your cool cars with kids around the world
- Order some extra LEGO pieces
- Find out if Sean is coming to your neighborhood and lots more!